MAY 2006

Markham Public Libraries
Milliken Mills Library
7600 Kennedy Road, Unit 1
Markham, ON L3R 9S5

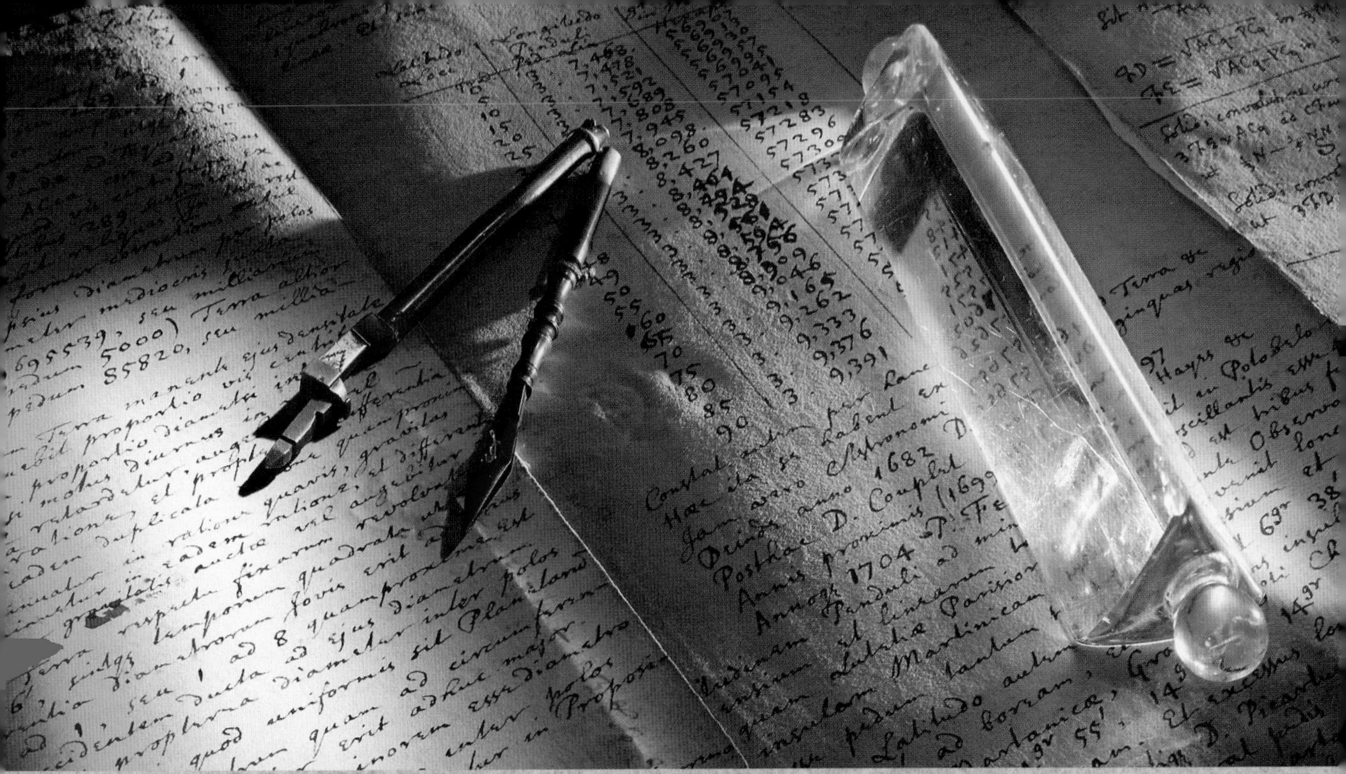

Primary Sources of Revolutionary Scientific Discoveries and Theories™

NEWTON AND THE THREE LAWS OF MOTION

Nicholas Croce

The Rosen Publishing Group, Inc., New York

Published in 2005 by The Rosen Publishing Group, Inc.
29 East 21st Street, New York, NY 10010

Copyright © 2005 by The Rosen Publishing Group, Inc.

First Edition

All rights reserved. No part of this book may be reproduced in any form without permission in writing from the publisher, except by a reviewer.

Library of Congress Cataloging-in-Publication Data

Croce, Nicholas.
Newton and the three laws of motion / Nicholas Croce.
p. cm. — (Primary sources of revolutionary scientific discoveries and theories)
Includes bibliographical references and index.
ISBN 1-4042-0311-7 (library binding)
1. Newton, Isaac, Sir, 1642–1727. 2. Motion.
I. Title. II. Series.
QC16.N7C72 2004
531'.11—dc22

2004004477

Printed in Hong Kong

On the front cover: The oil-on-canvas painting *Master Isaac Newton*, by Robert Hannah, 1905

On the back cover *(top to bottom)*: Nicolaus Copernicus, Charles Darwin, Edwin Hubble, Johannes Kepler, Gregor Mendel, Dmitry Mendeleyev, Isaac Newton, James Watson *(right)* and Francis Crick *(left)*

CONTENTS

INTRODUCTION

Isaac Newton was a brilliant scientist who lived during the seventeenth century. By the end of his career as a physicist, Newton had made some of the most important scientific discoveries the world had ever known, most notably the three laws of motion as well as the law of universal gravitation. Because of his work in the field of physics, Newton was praised for his brilliance, equally in mathematics and "natural philosophy," the name for science during Newton's age. Eventually, Newton achieved celebrity and was offered top teaching positions at the most prestigious schools in Europe.

THE PRICE OF GENIUS

Because of his success, Newton made many enemies—rival scientists who were jealous of his achievements. One of these scientists was the English physicist Robert Hooke, who claimed that Newton had stolen several of his ideas. One such idea eventually became the basis for Newton's three laws of motion, the work Newton is most remembered for. Soon after Newton's discovery of the three laws, several rival scientists came forward, each claiming Newton had stolen their ideas.

Angry and bitter, Newton was nearly driven mad trying to protect his ideas from others who were trying to profit from them. Newton eventually left science altogether at the height of his career. He soon embarked on an endeavor that seemed to

This photo, taken outside of Isaac Newton's home in Woolsthorpe, England, captures what is possibly the exact spot where the course of science would forever change. The tree pictured is most likely the offspring of the tree from which the famous apple fell. Legend states that an apple fell on Newton's head, which then led him to come up with the law of gravity. While this is not entirely true, the apple trees on Newton's estate certainly did influence the young genius's theories. Newton probably applied his observation of apples falling from trees to his existing theories. This would result in the universal law of gravitation. This law would explain gravity on Earth as well as how gravity worked in the farthest reaches of the universe.

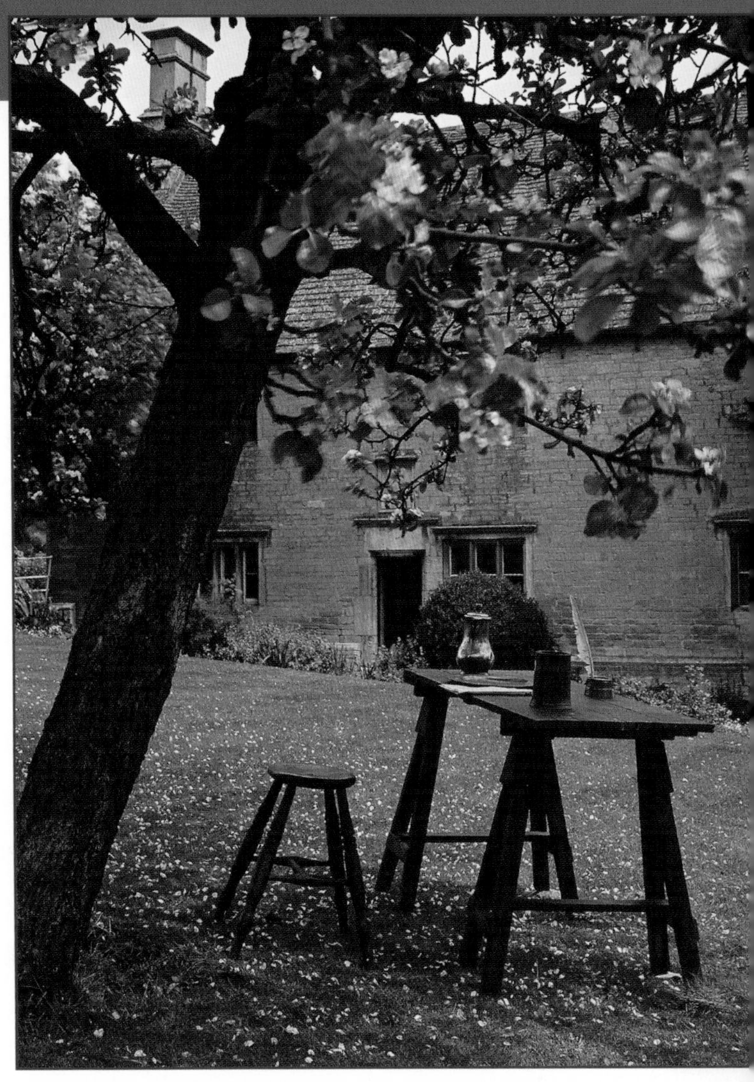

have nothing to do with his scientific talents: warden of the British Royal Mint.

There was very little that was scientific about Newton's new post, but genius cannot be held down for long. Soon after arriving at the mint, Newton developed an expertise in one crucial area—catching counterfeiters and thieves. He aided officials at the mint by enforcing strict disciplinary measures over the mint's employees. Newton's work sent many criminals to the gallows to be hanged, a punishment typical of the time for such an offense. Because of these harsh disciplinary practices, Newton was feared by criminals far and wide. Catching thieves and counterfeiters was quite a different role for Newton; he had been a reclusive scholar throughout his previous career as a scientist.

However, Isaac Newton was not satisfied disciplining would-be criminals. He developed a more successful method of stopping theft that was more in line with his personality as a man of the mind. Newton implemented the milling technique at the mint—applying ridges on the edges of coins to keep thieves from shaving off and reselling the precious metal from which these coins were once made.

The inspiration for Newton's brilliant method for stopping counterfeiting came from those scientists who he believed had been trying to take credit for his ideas. Although milling no longer serves any practical use because coins are no longer made of precious metal, it remains on certain coins today for artistic reasons.

If for no other purpose, milling should remind us that Isaac Newton paid the cost of scientific genius. It is evidence that he spent the remainder of his life fighting theft instead of answering the riddles of the universe. Newton's three laws of motion and the law of universal gravitation are among history's most important scientific discoveries. Therefore, it is understandable why others would want to be credited with his work. Newton's laws of motion gave the universe a sense of order at a time when its workings were still a mystery to most people. From the fall of an apple to the launch of a spacecraft, Newton's laws can be experienced by people in nearly all corners of life.

CHAPTER 1

BIOGRAPHY OF A GENIUS

Isaac Newton was a sickly baby, born in the small village of Woolsthorpe in Lincolnshire, England, on December 25, 1642. He was not even expected to survive his first day of life. His father had died three months earlier, so from birth, young Isaac had only his mother to care for him. Within two years, she married the wealthy minister Barnabas Smith and left Isaac to be raised by his grandmother. Isaac's mother did not return to him until Barnabas died nine years later in 1653. Isaac, indeed, did not have the best of childhoods, and many scholars argue that his troubled youth was responsible for the anxiety and insecurity the genius experienced throughout his years as an adult.

Trinity College

Newton left home to attend Trinity College in Cambridge, England, in June 1661. During this time, known as the Scientific Revolution, great advances in science were taking place. German astronomer Johannes Kepler (1571–1630) outlined the laws of planetary motion, and Italian scientist Galileo Galilei (1564–1642) was the first person to look into the farthest reaches of space using a telescope he created.

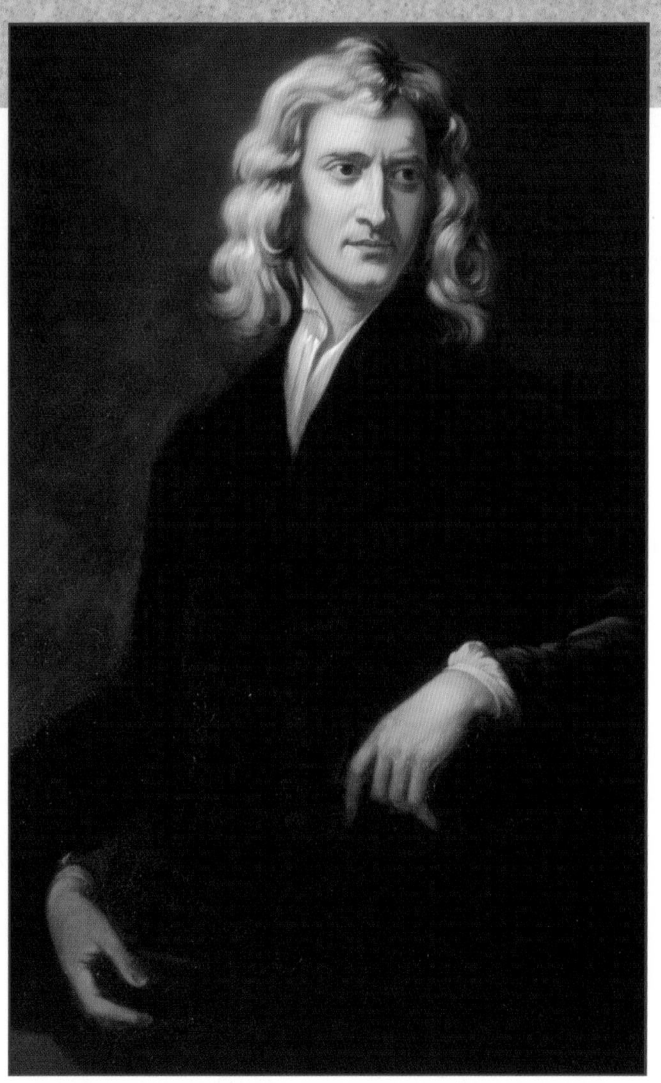

This painting, done by Hermann Goldschmidt in 1847 after an earlier painting done by Sir Godfrey Kneller, captures the genius Sir Isaac Newton in his prime. As a child, Newton did not show an outstanding brilliance. But at Trinity College, his genius blossomed. Even while a student at Trinity, Newton was publishing work that challenged the world of science. In 1665, while taking refuge from the plague at his family's estate in Woolsthorpe, England, Newton had the time to develop his ideas that would become the foundation for calculus. Also during this time, Newton began to experiment with optics (the study of light and matter) and gravitation (the attraction of matter to other matter).

At Trinity College, Newton studied the works of Aristotle, the ancient Greek philosopher and scientist. At the same time, Newton also began to study the works of new thinkers like French mathematician and scientist René Descartes. Both of these enlightened minds would have a great influence on the young genius.

Newton was so inspired by what he read that he published his own philosophies in 1664. *Quaestiones Quaedam Philosophicae* (Certain Philosophical Questions) begins with the now-famous line, "*Amicus Plato amicus Aristoteles magis amica veritas*." Translated from Latin, this phrase reads: "Plato is my friend, Aristotle is my friend, but my best friend is truth." What Newton meant by these words was that while he

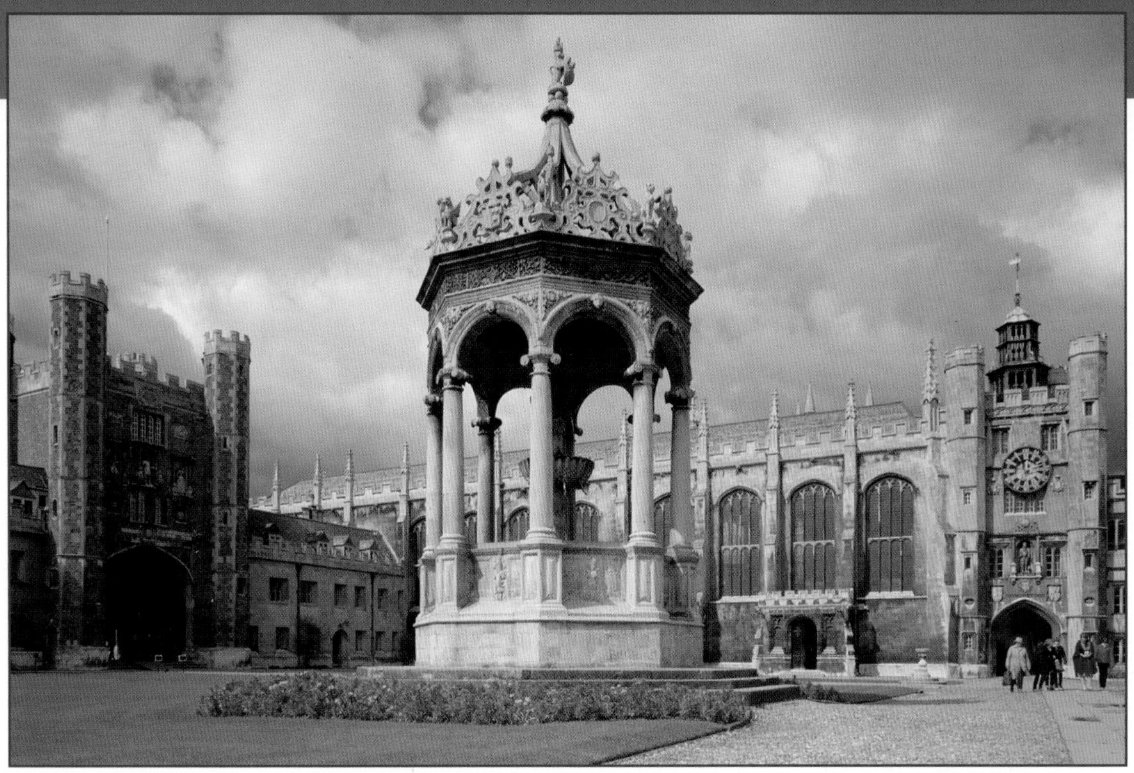

The Great Court is one of the highlights of the illustrious Trinity College in Cambridge, England. The college was founded in 1546 by King Henry VIII as part of the University of Cambridge. Famous graduates of Trinity include poet and philosopher Francis Bacon and poets Alfred, Lord Tennyson, Lord Byron, and William Makepeace Thackeray. While attending Trinity, Newton discovered great minds such as Aristotle, Galileo, and René Descartes.

respected the esteemed scientists of the past, he wanted to break new ground and make discoveries of his own.

With this newfound ambition, Newton left Trinity in April 1665 with a bachelor's degree. He would have continued with his education, but then disaster struck.

The Plague

The rapid spread of the deadly bubonic plague closed the doors of Trinity College almost immediately after Newton graduated. Called the black death because of the discoloration it formed on its victims, the bubonic plague swept through Europe, killing thousands in its path. English officials enforced rules to confine people to their homes in hopes of curbing the spread of the disease by limiting interaction between people. As a result, Newton was confined to his home for the next two years. This, however, gave Newton plenty of time to study. Unmarried and having few, if any, friends, Newton devoured books, especially those concerning science. Newton studied the various branches of mathematics, including algebra and geometry. He mastered these concepts in little more than a year, which is extremely fast.

Additionally, while the plague paralyzed England, Newton began thinking about motion. Newton studied the properties of motion and applied them to the movement of the moon and planets. From studying the motion of the planets, he developed the foundation for his theory of universal gravity.

The laws of motion that he discovered are still important today because the universe is in motion. Applying certain laws—truths that govern the way things move—Newton allows us to understand how the universe works. It is this study of the motion of objects that we call physics.

In 1669, Newton wrote *De Analysi per Aequationes Numeri Terminorum Infinitas* (On Analysis by Infinite Series). In this book, he outlined a new branch of mathematics, now known as calculus. When his theories reached the scientific community, Newton became famous overnight. Only a few years out of Trinity College, Newton was regarded as the leading mathematician in Europe.

Experimenting with Light

Light had been a great mystery to mankind. That was, until Newton began to study light as one of his great interests in addition to mathematics. Not even the leading scientific minds knew what

The earliest recorded use of the telescope was by Roger Bacon in the thirteenth century. However, the telescope was not widely used to search the heavens until the 1600s, when Galileo vastly improved the existing instruments. Before Newton, there existed only refracting telescopes, instruments that use lenses to focus light by bending it. In 1672, following his great work with optics, Newton built the first reflecting telescope. This instrument was much more accurate than its predecessor because it used mirrors to reflect light instead of bending and distorting it. Newton's first reflecting telescope is pictured here along with his manuscript pages from the *Principia Mathematica*.

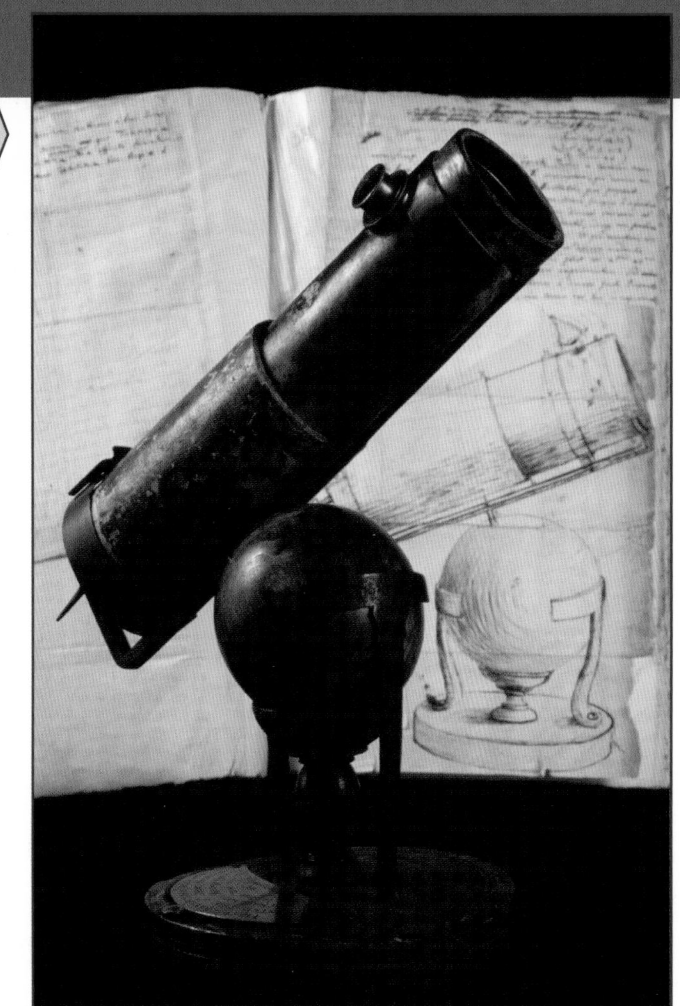

light was or how it worked. What causes colors? Why is the sky blue? Why can we see our reflection in a mirror? Not only was optics, the study of light, important in its own right, but discoveries in the behavior of light also changed the way people thought about other branches of science.

In 1666, Newton began to study light. Like many great scientific discoveries, the explanation of light stemmed from one person's curiosity. Newton wanted to learn what light was made of and how it worked. To conduct his studies, Newton bought a prism—a triangular piece of glass—at a local fair. He brought it home and placed it near a window through which a ray of sunlight shone. He noticed that the prism separated the sunlight into a rainbow of isolated colors. From this experiment, Newton discovered that natural light is made up of many different colors, which together make up the color spectrum. Each color had unique properties, such as its effect on the human eye. This effect enables people to see individual color.

However, there were several prominent scientists of the day who didn't agree with Newton about his discoveries about light. One scientist, Robert Hooke, considered himself a master in optics. Hooke's criticisms infuriated Newton. When Newton's paper *An Hypothesis Explaining the Properties of Light* was published in 1675, Hooke claimed that much of its content was stolen from him. This first accusation of theft by another scientist shook Newton to his core. In 1678, Newton had a nervous breakdown.

The *Principia*

By 1679, Newton had focused his attention on planetary orbits—the way in which planets move around the sun. Also by this time, Newton had outlined the three laws of motion as well as his theory of universal gravitation. Newton's theory of universal gravitation states that gravity is a force that exists throughout the universe and that its strength decreases in inverse (opposite) proportion to the square of the distance between two objects. Simply stated, this means that gravitational force decreases as objects move farther away from one another. From these ideas emerged Newton's *Philosophiae Naturalis Principia Mathematica* (Mathematical Principles of Natural Philosophy), or simply the *Principia*.

Begun many years earlier as a manuscript titled *De Motu Corporum in Gyrum* (On the Motion of Revolving Bodies), the *Principia* applied Newton's laws of motion and the theory of universal gravitation to the orbital motion of the planets. Newton

Philosophiae Naturalis Principia Mathematica, originally published in 1687, would become the cornerstone of modern physics. Pictured here is a page from an original edition, which today is housed at the Georgetown College Library in Washington, D.C. With encouragement and financial support from his colleague Edmond Halley, Newton was able to publish this major work. For the first time ever, the *Principia* would explain some of the most basic rules of physics. Most important, Newton's work outlined the laws of gravity, which affect everything in our universe, from falling apples to orbiting planets. (See page 54 for a transcription.)

[1]

PHILOSOPHIÆ
NATURALIS
Principia
MATHEMATICA

Definitiones.

Def. I.

Quantitas Materiæ eſt menſura ejuſdem orta ex illius Denſitate & Magnitudine conjunctim.

Aer duplo denſior in duplo ſpatio quadruplus eſt. Idem intellige de Nive et Pulveribus per compreſſionem vel liquefactionem condenſatis. Et par eſt ratio corporum omnium, quæ per cauſas quaſcunq; diverſimode condenſantur. Medii interea, ſi quod fuerit, interſtitia partium libere pervadentis, hic nullam rationem habeo. Hanc autem quantitatem ſub nomine corporis vel Maſſæ in ſequentibus paſſim intelligo. Innoteſcit ea per corporis cujuſq; pondus. Nam ponderi proportionalem eſſe reperi per experimenta pendulorum accuratiſſime inſtituta; uti poſthac docebitur.

B Def.

believed that the force holding the planets in their orbits must decrease the farther away the planet is from the sun. As Newton was applying this theory for calculating the orbit of the moon, he watched an apple fall from a tree. (Contrary to legend, the apple did not hit him on the head.) He made the connection: the force keeping the moon in orbit around the sun was quite possibly the same force that pulled the apple to the ground. He named this new force *gravitas* (gravity) after the Latin word for "heaviness."

The Gravity of Discovery

After the *Principia* was published, which announced Newton's groundbreaking work with gravity, Robert Hooke once again emerged to accuse Newton of thievery. Hooke's claim came from the fact that he had mentioned the idea of gravity to Newton some years before the publication of the *Principia*. However, Hooke had never proven the theory. As a result, Newton lashed out and deleted all references to Hooke in a later edition of the *Principia*, which further fueled the ongoing rivalry between the two scientists.

Though Newton's mind was preoccupied with Hooke's charge of plagiarism, Newton had other things to distract him. The *Principia* raised Newton to international fame. Scientists all over the world who fervently followed Newton named themselves Newtonians. Newton was also becoming popular with women. He soon found himself surrounded by numerous female scientists. This formerly reclusive man's only prior contacts with women were his mother and niece. But the fame soon got to Newton, and he began to lose interest in his scientific and mathematical pursuits. In 1696, nine years after publishing the *Principia*, he abandoned science and accepted the job of warden of the British Royal Mint.

For the remaining years of his life, Newton gained numerous awards for his lifelong achievements. In 1703, he was elected president of the Royal Society, a prestigious British academy of science. In 1705, Queen Anne of Great Britain knighted him, which was the first time in history a scientist had been given the honor.

Newton continued to revise his work and publish updated editions as well. In 1706, he published a Latin edition of *Opticks*, which outlined his study of light; a second English edition was issued in 1718. Though he continued to work both for the mint and for the Royal Society, Newton had clearly passed his glory days. He presided at the meetings of the Royal Society but was often found dozing off. Newton died in London on March 20, 1727, wealthy with the fortune he had amassed at the mint.

Newton's life was filled with its share of highs and lows. He is remembered as one of the greatest scientists to have ever lived, only to regret the fame that came with this praise. He established a new set of rules by which the universe works, only to be called a plagiarizer as a result. In the coming chapters, we will learn exactly why Newton's laws of motion were so revolutionary, from the chaotic times in which he lived to the effects his laws had on later scientists.

CHAPTER 2

THE SCIENTIFIC REVOLUTION

Before the Scientific Revolution (fifteenth through seventeenth centuries), the Roman Catholic Church was highly esteemed and very powerful in European society. Being such, the church explained anything that was unknown about the universe. Why is there day and night? Why does the sun rise in the east and set in the west? Why does the moon have phases? According to the Catholic Church, these questions all had one simple answer: they were the work of God. As a result, there wasn't much need for scientific questioning.

For several centuries leading up to the Scientific Revolution, the day-to-day lifestyle of Europeans had not improved. There was little fertile land on which to grow crops, and where there was land, it was not used very efficiently. Large unusable forests covered the land, and malaria, a deadly disease, was common. The population was small and grew very slowly, not exceeding 5 million on the island of Great Britain. (Today, Great Britain's population approaches 60 million.) The food was not nutritious, and pestilence and famine were common.

When the Scientific Revolution began, great advances in science swept across Europe. Scientist after scientist made landmark discoveries or greatly improved upon a predecessor's work. It was a time of scientific brainstorming in which some of the universe's greatest riddles were answered. With these advances in science, people began to see the world as they had never seen it before. Ordinary people saw the universe as an ordered and predictable place, whereas before, it was seen as a disorganized system controlled only by the whims of God.

The Geocentric Model

Although many historians believe that the Scientific Revolution began during Newton's time, many argue that it officially began in the year 1543. Before this time, it was commonly accepted that Earth was the center of the universe—a theory known as the geocentric (Earth-centered) system. This theory was widely accepted mainly because the church supported it. In 1543, however, Polish astronomer Nicolaus Copernicus argued that Earth was not the center of the universe. In fact, Copernicus believed, the sun was the center of the universe.

Copernicus's died in the year 1543. His manuscript *De Revolutionibus Orbium Coelestium* (On the Revolutions of Heavenly Spheres) had just been published, outlining his system that the sun, and not Earth, was the center of the universe. This would become known as the heliocentric (sun-centered) system. Earth, Copernicus argued, as well as the rest of the planets, revolved around the sun. Copernicus's system contradicted the dominant model of the motion of the universe, which the Roman Catholic Church supported.

The church's explanation of the geocentric model followed the Ptolemaic model. Named after second-century Egyptian astronomer Claudius Ptolemaeus, or Ptolemy, the Ptolemaic model explained that the planets moved in a back-and-forth

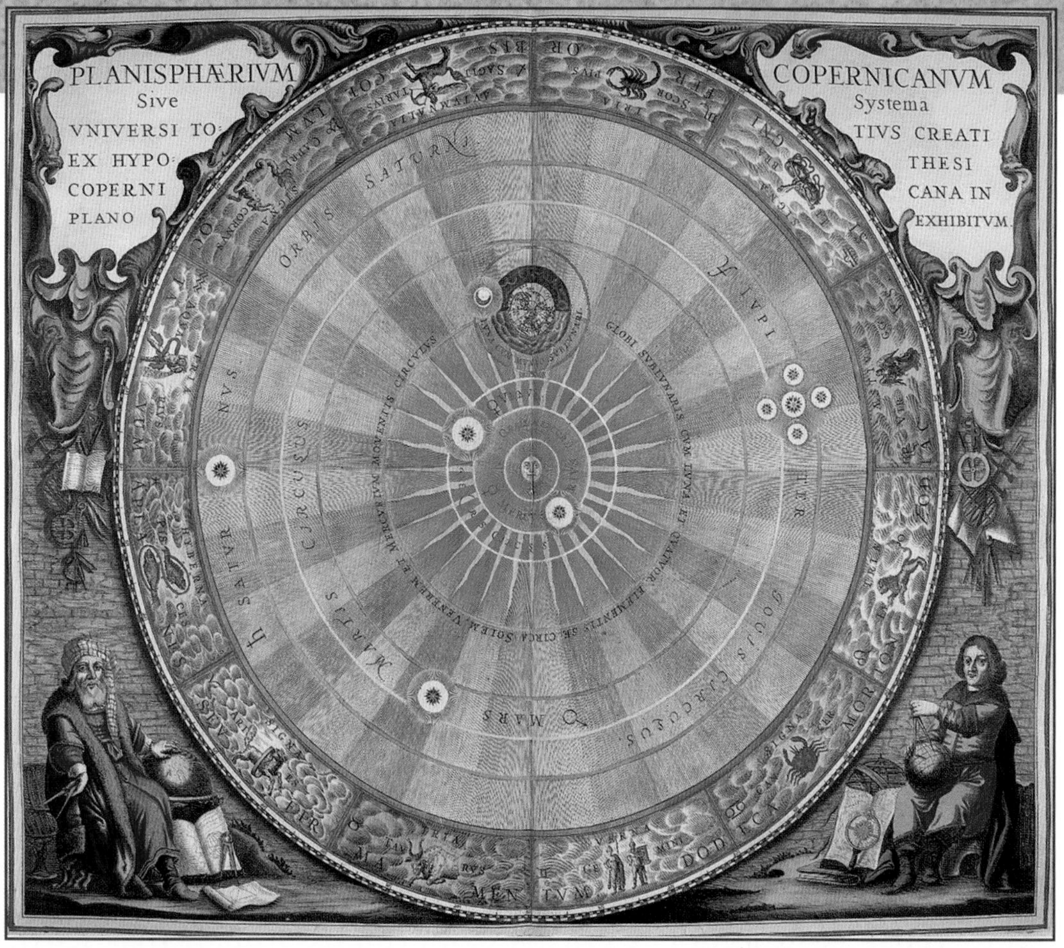

For centuries, people believed Earth was the center of the universe. It wasn't until 1543 that Nicolaus Copernicus challenged this belief and put forth the idea that the sun is the center of the universe. This hand-colored engraving from the sixteenth century depicts Copernicus's revolutionary idea.

motion while the stars moved in a straight line across the heavens. The Ptolemaic model of the universe did not make much sense to scientists and average people alike, mostly because there were several oddities that were never explained. However, the model had gone unchallenged for thirteen centuries because the church accepted it.

To the Roman Catholic Church, the belief in a heliocentric system was heretical, or against the church's beliefs. Heretics were severely punished and oftentimes killed. After Copernicus published his work, many people began to question the church's doctrines. They thought, if Earth wasn't the center of the universe, what else was the church wrong about? Could the church be depended on to answer the questions of the universe? Who was able to give more reliable answers? Scientists or church leaders? Thanks in part to Copernicus, many questions would soon follow, and the Scientific Revolution would begin in earnest.

The Laws of Planetary Motion

In 1609, Johannes Kepler published his book *Astronomia Nova* (New Astronomy). According to Kepler, the planets move around the sun in elliptical, or oval, paths, rather than in circular orbits. Expanding on Copernicus's findings, Kepler offered this as further proof of the heliocentric model.

Specifically, Kepler calculated three laws that describe how the planets orbit the sun. Instead of traveling in circles as thought earlier, the planets traveled in these ellipses with the sun at one focus. This was his first law. Kepler's second law states that the time needed for a planet to travel over any specific section of the orbit is proportional to the area between that section and the sun. The third law states that there is a relationship between the square of the planet's orbital period and the cube of the radius of its orbit. Simply stated, the second and third laws explain that the velocity of a planet increases as it moves closer to the sun.

Kepler's proof that the planets revolve around the sun strengthened the theory of the heliocentric solar system. Kepler's laws also furthered the notion that the universe was quite an ordered place, a place that could be mathematically

Galileo Galilei was one of the greatest minds of the Scientific Revolution and is known as the father of modern astronomy. Among Galileo's many contributions to science is his discovery of the moons of Jupiter and the phases of Venus, and that the sun has sunspots. Like Copernicus a century before him, Galileo questioned the doctrines of the Catholic Church and put forth ideas that forever changed the world. The work of Galileo would have a major influence on young Isaac Newton. Some of Galileo's astronomical observations would lay the groundwork for Newton's universal law of gravitation. This drawing of Galileo was done by Ottavio Mario Leoni in the early seventeenth century.

and scientifically explained. This new view of the universe gave people the sense that there was much more to explore and learn.

Observing the Heavens

In 1609, Italian astronomer Galileo Galilei read Kepler's *Astronomia Nova* and was very impressed. That same year, Galileo bought a tool recently invented by the Dutch that allowed people to visually explore the vast reaches of space—the telescope. Galileo then built his own three-powered telescope, which magnified objects up to three times. He then built an eight-powered telescope. Through his experiments, Galileo

One of Galileo's major contributions to astronomy was his vast improvement on existing telescopes. Before Galileo's work, telescopes could only magnify objects three times. By the early seventeenth century, Galileo had invented a telescope that could magnify objects eight times, and he later developed a telescope that could magnify objects twenty times. Galileo turned his telescopes toward the heavens and was the first to effectively use the instrument to see into the far reaches of the solar system. Pictured at right is one of Galileo's telescopes, which today is housed at the Museo di Storia della Scienza in Florence, Italy. Newton would later improve upon Galileo's telescopes by creating the first reflecting telescope, which used mirrors.

learned lens grinding, which is the art of making special lenses for telescopes. He continued to make telescopes that were increasingly more powerful.

In the fall of that year, Galileo pointed toward the heavens his latest telescope, which magnified objects twenty times. He observed the moon in all of its phases over several weeks and sketched what he saw. At that time, most astronomers assumed that the moon was made up of gases and formed a perfect sphere. What Galileo saw, however, was a cratered, rocky surface that was imperfect, much like that of Earth.

Then in January 1610, Galileo observed four moons orbiting Jupiter and described his findings in *Sidereus Nuncius* (The

Sidereal Messenger). Galileo later discovered the rings of Saturn and the fact that Venus has phases much like Earth's moon.

These discoveries were revolutionary. The cratered surface of the moon showed that the universe was not perfect as previously believed. The moons of Jupiter showed that there was more than one center of motion in the universe. The phases of Venus proved that the planet revolved around the sun, strengthening the idea of Copernicus's heliocentric system.

Galileo supported the heliocentric system. And like Copernicus, Galileo was questioned by the leaders of the Catholic Church. Galileo went to Rome to defend himself and his theories. As a result, he was ordered by Cardinal Robert Bellarmine to keep quiet about his discoveries. Bellarmine instructed him "not to hold, teach, or defend" the Copernican system "in any way whatever, either orally or in writing."

Galileo moved on, however. In 1624, he returned to Rome and met with Pope Urban VIII, the head of the Catholic Church. Though the pope gave Galileo permission to write a book on his findings, he would only allow it on one condition: that Galileo treat his theories as if they were fiction, not what he believed to be scientific fact. By receiving the pope's permission and agreeing to the terms, Galileo avoided the charge of heresy. Galileo agreed, and in 1630, he completed *Dialogo Sopra i Due Massimi Sistemi del Mondo, Tolemaico e Copernicano* (Dialogue Concerning the Two Chief World Systems, Ptolemaic and Copernican).

Upon completion, Galileo sent the manuscript to a censor in Rome to check it for any signs that it went against the church's teachings. Because of an outbreak of the plague, communication between Florence, where Galileo was, and Rome was slow. So to speed up the process, Galileo requested that a censor in Florence read the manuscript. Though the censor had many criticisms of the book, he allowed it to be published, but only after Galileo wrote a clear introduction stating that the book was a completely fictional account. The *Dialogue* first appeared in Florence in 1632. Although Galileo made concessions to the doctrines of Catholicism, his work was still controversial and angered much of the church. As a result, Galileo was placed under house arrest, where he remained until his death in 1642.

Galileo's story is an example of the spirit of the Scientific Revolution, when truth was more important than anything else, even religion. Scientists such as Galileo fought to have the truth exposed at any cost, even if it required cloaking it as fiction.

It was this passion and energy that Newton inherited from Galileo. Newton also inherited a wealth of knowledge gained by his predecessors that he would use as a springboard for his own experimentation. He took these discoveries and applied an order and system to them. As he wrote in a letter to Robert Hooke on February 5, 1675, "If I have seen further [than certain other men] it is by standing upon the shoulders of giants."

CHAPTER 3

THE PATH TO DISCOVERY

His friends at Cambridge all agreed: Newton was a genius. Newton's friend William Whitson once said, "Sir Isaac, in mathematics, could sometimes see almost by intuition." But while Newton mastered the works of the most advanced mathematicians of his day, his curiosity for the discipline was not satisfied.

Algebra is good for figuring out the answers to simple equations. And geometry is good for understanding simple problems dealing with spatial relations. But what about the more complex problems—ones that Newton imagined while gazing at the heavens?

How could one figure out the speed of a moving object, such as a tossed ball? How does its path change as its velocity changes?

When the ball is thrown up, it is constantly slowing down. Once it reaches its highest point in the air, the ball starts to fall. As it falls, it speeds up, but the angle at which it falls depends on how fast it's going. The faster it goes, the greater its arc. The slower it goes, the smaller its arc. Here, the unknown factors are the ball's position and speed. How does one calculate these things?

Newton's *On Analysis by Infinite Series* was written in 1669 but not published until two years later, when it eventually circulated as a manuscript. The landmark text was not published as a book until 1711. This title page is from a 1736 publication of the book. As groundbreaking as this work was, it was only the beginning for Isaac Newton. While Newton and Gottfried Wilhelm Leibniz worked out methods for fluxions independently, Newton's were far superior. As in Newton's feud with Robert Hooke, Leibniz also accused Newton of plagiarism. The feud between the two men was unique because of its intensity and also because it was extremely public. (See page 54 for a transcription.)

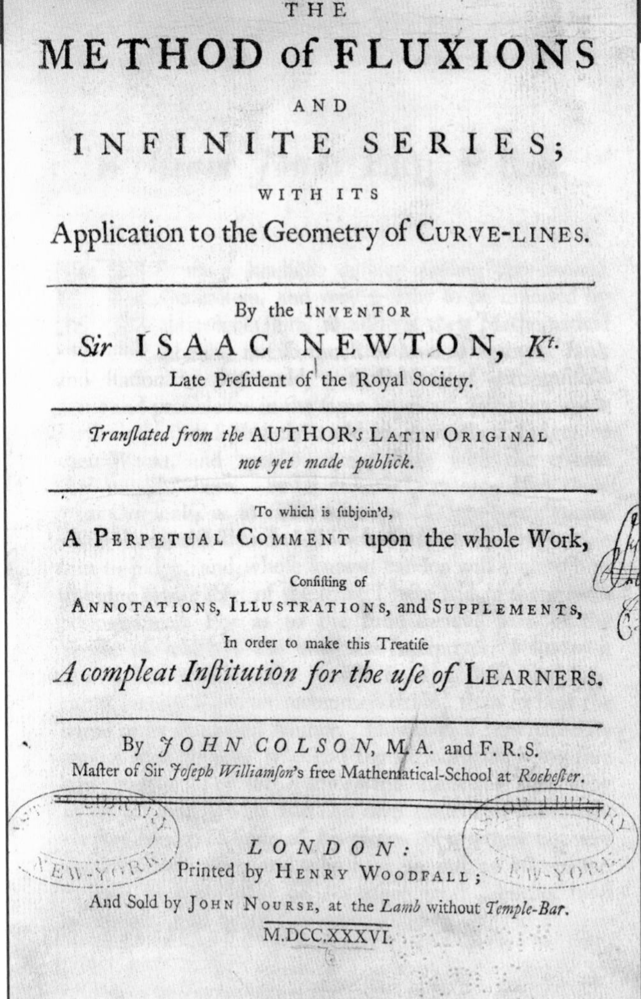

THE

METHOD of FLUXIONS

AND

INFINITE SERIES;

WITH ITS

Application to the Geometry of CURVE-LINES.

By the INVENTOR

Sir ISAAC NEWTON, *K^t.*

Late Preſident of the Royal Society.

Tranſlated from the AUTHOR'*s* LATIN ORIGINAL *not yet made publick.*

To which is ſubjoin'd,

A PERPETUAL COMMENT upon the whole Work,

Conſiſting of

ANNOTATIONS, ILLUSTRATIONS, and SUPPLEMENTS,

In order to make this Treatiſe

A compleat Inſtitution for the uſe of LEARNERS.

By *JOHN COLSON*, M. A. and F. R. S.

Maſter of Sir *Joſeph Williamſon's* free Mathematical-School at *Rocheſter.*

LONDON:

Printed by HENRY WOODFALL;

And Sold by JOHN NOURSE, at the *Lamb* without *Temple-Bar.*

M.DCC.XXXVI.

Calculus

Newton was only twenty-three years old when he came up with the idea of "fluxions," what is now called calculus. During the same time, a German philosopher named Gottfried Wilhelm Leibniz was developing similar ideas. While many historians argue who developed their ideas first, both Newton and Leibniz are credited with laying the groundwork for calculus.

Calculus deals with calculations that are constantly changing, such as the speed and position of a ball that is thrown. But Newton's calculus didn't deal with just the mathematics of a tossed ball. He could apply his mathematics to the motion of any object in the universe.

Newton imagined the ball being shot from a cannon. With a strong enough charge in the cannon, the ball could be shot into outer space. But it would still be pulled to Earth by gravity. The only difference is that the ball was shot so far away that it fell into orbit around Earth, much like how the moon orbits Earth. The ball is orbiting Earth at so great a speed that it never reaches Earth's surface. In effect, it falls past Earth. Newton's calculus explained the physics of the universe. Everything from the motion of the tossed ball to the orbit of the moon follows these physical laws.

In 1669, Newton wrote *De Analysi per Aequationes Numeri Terminorum Infinitas* (On Analysis by Infinite Series), summarizing his findings. The book was circulated among a select group of scholars and immediately sparked interest. Its success is what made Newton known as a leading mind in mathematics.

The Composition of Light

Around this same time, Newton was conducting experiments in an area of study that seemed unrelated—light.

During the seventeenth century, many people believed that colors were modifications of white light, or that colors come from white light. Newton proved that white light is really a combination of all the colors in the spectrum.

After Newton bought a prism at the local fair, he shone a beam of sunlight through it. He did this by drilling a one-eighth inch hole in the shutter of his bedroom window. The light shone through the shutter, then through the prism, and onto the opposite wall. To Newton's surprise, the light appeared in the form of all the colors in the spectrum, separated one from another.

Just to be sure that he was properly conducting this experiment, he placed a second prism in the path of the ray of light,

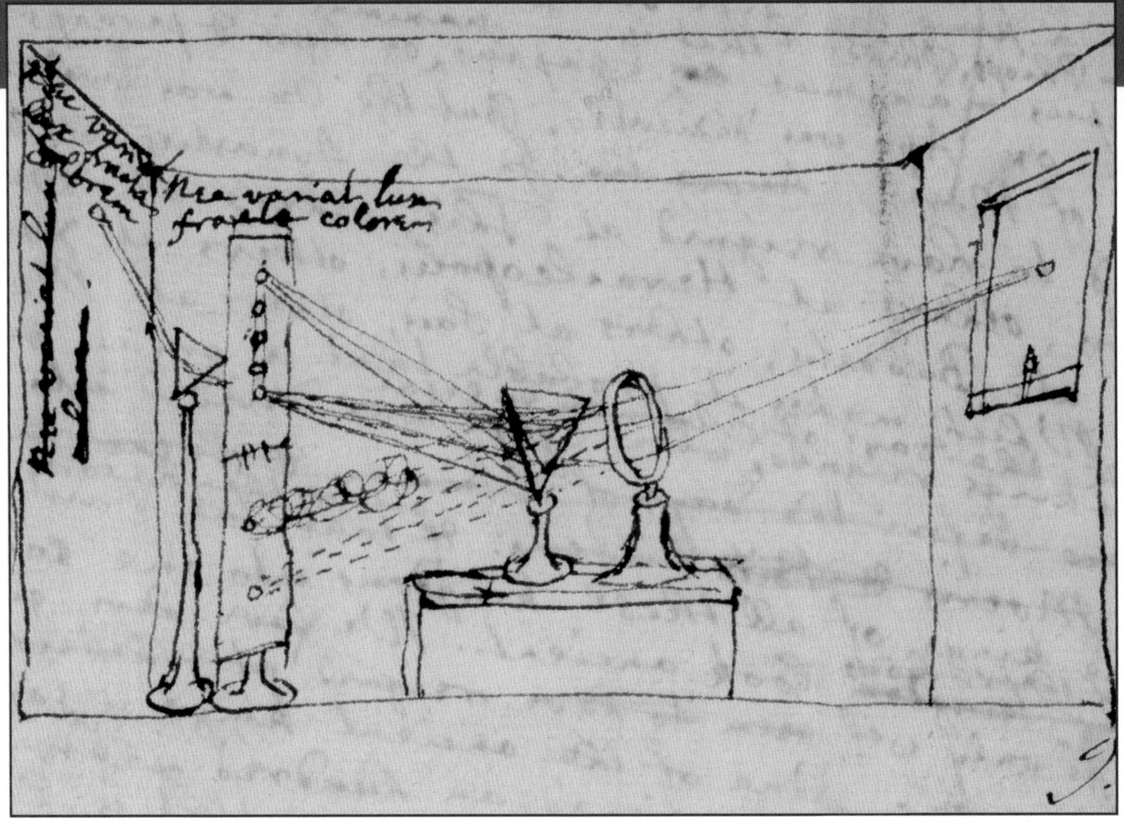

A page from Isaac Newton's notebook shows an original sketch demonstrating his experiment for determining the composition of white light. For this experiment, Newton drilled a hole in the shutter of his window, allowing a small ray of sunlight to enter the room and focus on a prism. The prism then reflected the "white" sunlight and separated it into the colors of the color spectrum. From this, Newton deduced that white light is made up of many different colors. This experiment would directly lead to Newton's creation of the reflecting telescope.

then a third. This increased the prism's ability to separate those colors that now shone on the wall into the white light that scientists of the day believed they were made of. Each of the colors remained unchanged, which proved that the colors were not composed of white light. On the contrary, Newton's experiment proved that white light is composed of all the colors in the spectrum, much like a rainbow. Newton, as he said, "untwisted the shining robe of day."

Newton's studies showed that since the behavior of light follows scientific principles, the universe is an ordered, predictable, and mechanical place. If the movement of light could be explained with a mathematical equation, then why not the movement of the moon and the planets?

Universal Gravitation

In late 1679, Robert Hooke contacted Newton. Through a series of letters, Hooke mentioned to Newton that he was studying planetary motion, or the way planets revolve around the sun. Newton explained to Hooke that he, too, had been conducting experiments that would illustrate the rotation of Earth. Newton suggested dropping an object from a tower. If Earth were moving, the speed at the top of the tower would be greater than that at the base. A spinning bicycle wheel also illustrates this point—the speed of the outside edge of the wheel is greater than that of the axle. Since the top of the tower has a greater velocity than the bottom, the object wouldn't fall to the ground in a straight line, but would fall slightly to one side.

Newton further illustrated his point by suggesting that if the object were allowed to fall through Earth, it would spiral around the center until it came to a stop. This, Hooke pointed out, was wrong. According to Hooke's studies of planetary motion, the object wouldn't come to a stop at the center. It would pass through the center and come back to its original location in an elliptical orbit. Newton didn't like being corrected.

Newton wrote back, correcting Hooke's calculations by using the assumption that gravity is constant, or that it has the same strength everywhere in the universe. Hooke countered with the suggestion that gravity was not constant but that its strength

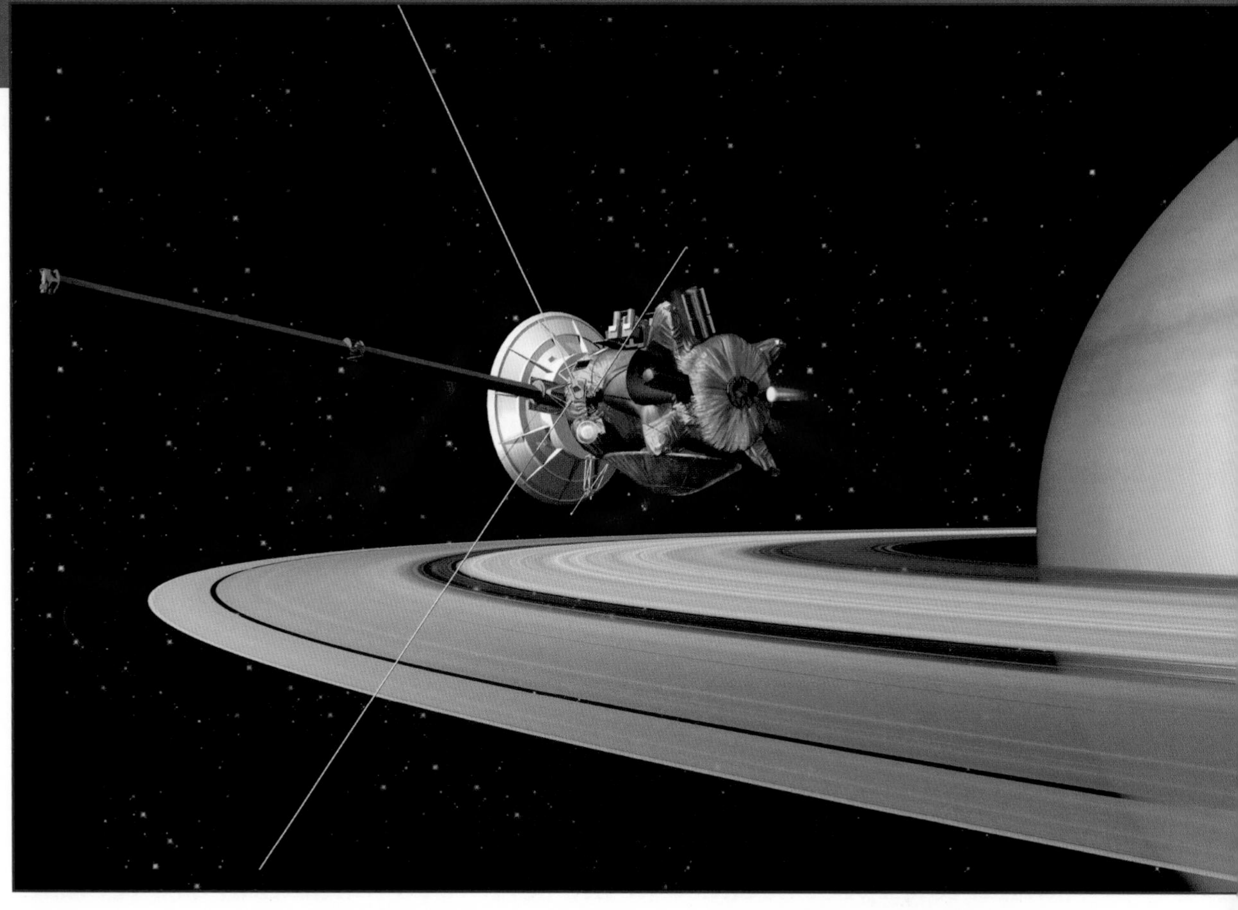

Newton's law of gravity has been applied to deep space exploration. This artist's rendering captures the movement of the *Cassini* space probe, a NASA spacecraft that reached Saturn's rings in the summer of 2004. *Cassini* will employ Newton's law and create a gravitational "slingshot," which will propel the satellite around Saturn, taking advantage of Saturn's own gravitational forces. According to Newton, the same law of gravity that applies to a simple apple falling from a tree here on Earth is the same law that applies to objects in deep space.

decreases the farther the object is from the source of gravity. Specifically, the force of gravity decreases with inverse, or opposite, proportion to the square of the distance between the two objects. According to Hooke, when two objects move away from each other, the strength of gravity between them decreases by a square of their distance. This was a key point. This exchange continued for several years.

By early 1684, English astronomer Edmond Halley was having similar conversations about gravity with both Hooke and English architect Sir Christopher Wren. Halley suggested that the force of gravity decreases with distance. To his excitement, Hooke said that he had come to the same conclusion. The problem, of course, was proving it mathematically, which no one had ever done.

As an incentive, Wren offered to give a valuable book to whoever of the two men could solve the problem. Hooke, in his proud manner, said that he already knew the answer but was keeping it a secret until he decided to make it public. In turn, Halley called upon Newton to see if he could solve the problem.

Halley boarded a train from London to Cambridge in August 1684. Having met Newton only once before, Halley didn't know what to expect because of the scientist's reputation as a recluse. But Newton was happy to see him.

After talking for a while, Halley asked Newton the question he had come a long way to ask: what kind of curve "would be described by the planets supposing the force of attraction towards the sun to be reciprocal to the square of their distances from it?" To Halley's surprise, Newton had the same conclusion that he, Hooke, and Wren had come to. Newton answered that gravity decreases with inverse proportion to the square of the distances between the two objects. Halley was greatly surprised when he asked Newton how he had come to that conclusion. Newton replied simply, "I have calculated it."

CHAPTER 4

THE EUREKA MOMENT

To Halley's delight, his curiosity about how Newton solved the problem would soon be satisfied. But to Halley's disappointment, Newton had lost his notes. Nevertheless, Newton promised to rewrite his notes and send them to Halley once they were complete. For the next eleven months, Newton rewrote his calculations for elliptical orbits. Finally, in November 1684, he sent Halley the first copy of *De Motu Corporum in Gyrum* (On the Motion of Revolving Bodies).

Halley was amazed. This was the first paper published on the relationship between motion and the energy and forces that influence it. Halley so believed in the importance of *De Motu* that he visited Newton again to ask if he could present the paper before the Royal Society as well as publish it. Newton agreed.

Newton's paper was well received by the Royal Society. Halley was urged to persuade Newton to publish it as soon as possible. For the next year and a half, Newton prepared *De Motu* for publication. Newton presented the first third of the manuscript to the Royal Society. It was so well received that the society offered to pay to publish *De Motu*, but the members soon realized that the society was out of money. In the end, Halley himself financed

tertiam, X longitudinem quam Cometa toto illo tempore ea cum velocitate quam habet in mediocri Telluris à Sole distantia, describere posset, & tV perpendiculum in chordam $T\tau$. In longitudine media tB sumatur utcunque punctum B, & inde versus Solem S

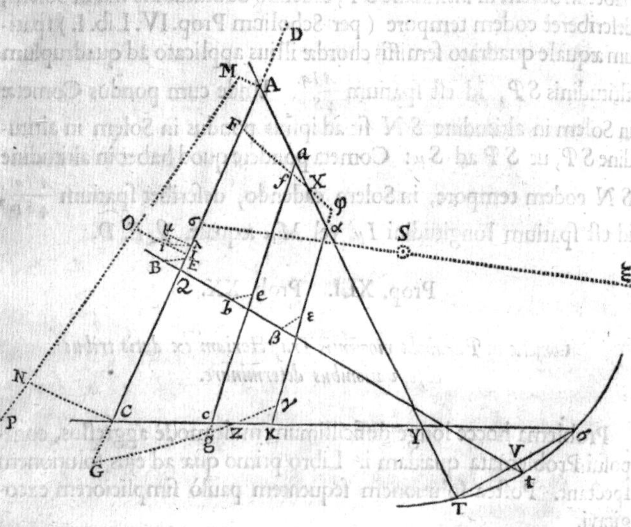

ducatur linea BE, quæ sit ad Sagittam tV ut contentum sub SB & St quadrato ad cubum hypotenusæ trianguli rectanguli, cujus latera sunt SB & tangens latitudinis Cometæ in observatione secunda ad radium tB. Et per punctum E agatur recta AEC, cujus partes AE, EC ad rectas TA & τC terminatæ, sint ad invicem ut tempora V & W: Tum per puncta A, B, C, duc circumferentiam circuli, eamque biseca in i, ut & chordam AC in I. Age occultam Si secantem AC in λ, & comple parallelogrammum $iI\lambda\mu$. Cape $I\sigma$ æqualem $3I\lambda$, & per Solem S age occultam $\sigma\xi$ æqualem $3S\sigma + 3i\lambda$. Et deletis jam literis A, E, C, I, à puncto B versus punctum ξ duc occultam

Newton's *Principia* might not have been written were it not for a furious competition between Newton and Robert Hooke. Hooke was unable to prove Kepler's laws. Newton then took up the problem and proved them in his groundbreaking *De Motu Corporum in Gyrum* (On the Motion of Revolving Bodies). Later, Newton would expand on *De Motu* for the *Principia*. The massive book contains countless problems and diagrams split up into three different books. In the third, and most important, book, "The Systems of the World," Newton applied his law of gravitation to the motion of planets, the moon, and comets. The page at left describes the complicated motion of a comet as explained by the law of gravitation. (See page 55 for a transcription.)

the project. In its final form, *De Motu* was published with the title *Philosophiae Naturalis Principia Mathematica* (Mathematical Principles of Natural Philosophy), or simply the *Principia*. Today, many scientists believe that the *Principia* is the most important text ever written in the history of science. The *Principia* explains physics in three basic laws, plus the ideas expressed in the work gave order to the universe at a time when people believed the universe was a disorderly place.

The Book That Nobody Understood

The *Principia* was published in July 1687, and it is composed of three books. Book I explains the concept of motion without friction. Book II concerns the motion of fluids and the effect of friction on solid bodies moving in fluids. Book III is considered the most profound and what made the *Principia* an important text. It covers Newton's famed three laws of motion and the law of universal gravitation.

The Three Laws

Newton's first law states, "Every body [object] continues in its state of rest, or of uniform motion in a straight line, unless it is compelled to change that state by forces impressed upon it." This was not an original idea—Galileo first thought of it nearly fifty years earlier. But Newton incorporated Galileo's theory to involve the behavior of matter, namely the movement of the planets.

According to the first law, however, the planets would not circle the sun but rather move in a continuous straight line out into space. The second law explains why this doesn't happen.

"The change of motion," the second law reads, "is proportional to the motive force impressed; and is made in the direction of the straight line in which that force is impressed." Simply stated, the reason the planets do not continue in a straight line is because they are continually pulled toward the sun by the sun's immense gravity. This is demonstrated by swinging a ball on a string. The ball keeps circling around because of the string's pull, or effect, on it. In this example, the string represents gravity.

Newton's third law states, "To every action there is always opposed an equal reaction: or, the mutual action of two bodies upon each other are always equal, and directed to contrary parts." Newton devised this law in its entirety. In simpler terms, the third law states that if one body pulls on another, the other body is pulling with the same amount of force. For

This portrait, done by Sir James Thornhill in 1710, depicts Sir Isaac Newton as an elder statesman. Newton's astonishing achievements led to worldwide fame, which brought its own problems. Plagued by both critics and jealous peers, Newton became increasingly frustrated and disappointed with science. By the time of this portrait's creation, Newton had all but left the world of science and taken the post as warden of the British Royal Mint. However, Newton did remain a figure in science by acting as president of the Royal Society. Like most great visionaries, what matters most is what is left behind. Newton's contributions to science undoubtedly changed the world forever.

example, Earth pulls on the moon, and in turn, the moon pulls on Earth with an equal amount of force. The reason the moon orbits the Earth rather than the other way around is due to the fact that Earth is so much more massive than the moon. Therefore, Earth has more gravity.

In addition to the three laws of motion, Newton's law of universal gravitation states that every object in the universe is acting on every other object. As Newton writes in Proposition VII of Book III, "Every particle of matter attracts every other particle with a force proportional to the products of the masses and inversely proportional to the square of the distances between them." This theory declares that the gravity of everything in the universe affects the movement and position of every other

This copper engraved print demonstrates the romantic environment of Gresham College during the eighteenth century. The Royal Society was founded at Gresham on November 28, 1660, as a direct result of the Scientific Revolution to help foster some of the greatest scientific minds in the world. Founding members of the society include Christopher Wren, Robert Boyle, and Robert Hooke. In 1710, during the presidency of Sir Isaac Newton, the society moved to its permanent home on Crane Court in London. Today, the society still plays an important role in promoting natural and applied sciences around the world.

thing. Anything with mass, from the sun to a grain of sand, has its own gravity and influence on the rest of the universe.

This was a mind-boggling concept in Newton's time; even some people today find it difficult to understand. At the time, gravity was thought only as having an effect on the sun, moon, and planets. But with Newton's law of universal gravitation, he showed that every body in the universe, from the smallest to the largest, has gravitational influence. In *As You Like It*, English playwright William Shakespeare described all of humanity: "All the world's a stage, and all the men and women merely players." So, too, Newton described the nature of the entire universe, that every object in it plays a role.

Universal Fame

Many people, both common and academic, did not understand concepts presented in the *Principia*, but Newton's instant fame proved that the general public sensed his work was revolutionary. As quoted in *Isaac Newton: The Greatest Scientist of All Time*, one student remarked while passing the scientist on the street, "There goes the man that writt a book that neither he nor anybody else understands." Dr. Humphrey Babington, a Trinity College scholar, suggested that even educated people "might study seven years before they understood anything of it." Despite the criticism, Newtonians filled the teaching positions at England's most prominent schools, such as Oxford, Cambridge, and Gresham College, teaching the laws of the universe.

CHAPTER 5

THE LAWS EXPLAINED

Although the subject matter behind the *Principia* may have baffled the general public of the seventeenth century, Newton's three laws of motion are in fact deceptively simple. When one hits a baseball, pedals a bike, or pushes a friend on a swing, one of Newton's three laws is at work. But what most people don't realize is that the law that applies to the physics of hitting a baseball is the same one that applies to spacecraft exploring the farthest reaches of space. The laws of physics behind pedaling a bicycle are the same laws that propel rockets into space. The physics of pushing a friend on a swing is basically the same as one of the physical laws that keeps Earth in rotation, giving us night and day.

Newton's three laws can be applied almost anywhere in the universe, making them, as the term suggests, universal. This universality is what makes Newton's laws so brilliant and considered by many as among the most important scientific discoveries ever. Let's explore them in more depth.

The First Law

In the *Principia*, Newton explained his first law of motion as such: "Every body [object] continues in its state of rest, or of uniform

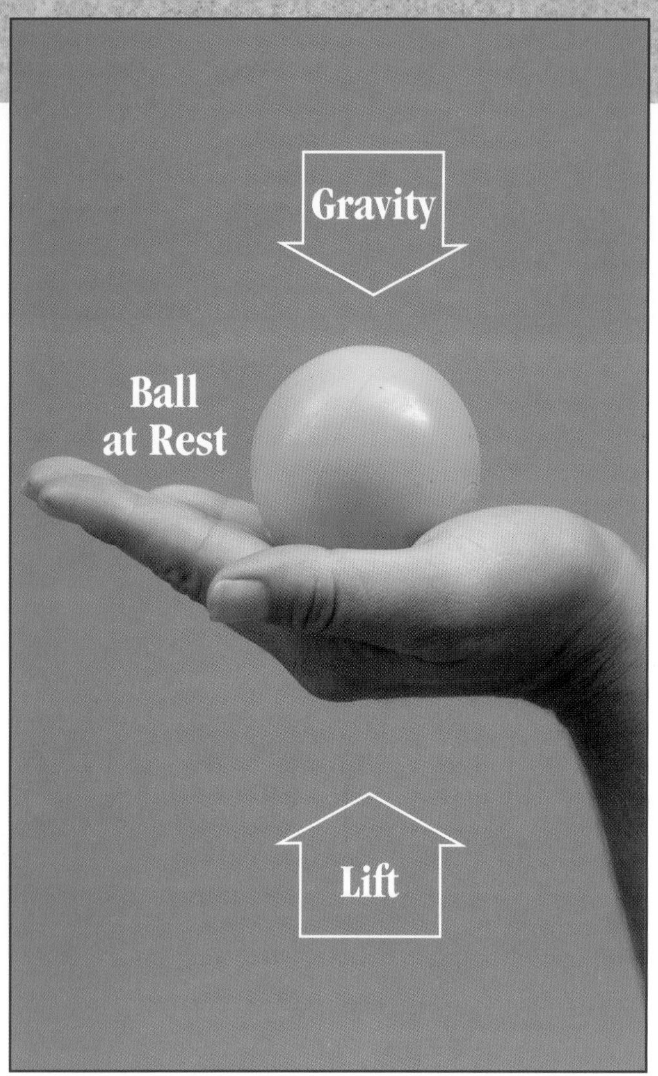

Newton's first law of motion states, in simple terms, that objects at rest tend to stay at rest and objects in motion tend to stay in motion, unless acted upon by an outside force. This diagram demonstrates this first law and the effect gravity has on objects here on Earth. If you hold a ball in your hand, the ball is at rest. However, while the ball is at rest, it is still being acted upon by the two forces of gravity and lift. The force of gravity is pulling the ball down, while your hand is lifting the ball in order to hold it up. As you hold the ball still, the two forces are in perfect balance. Let go of the ball, or lift the ball, and the forces become unbalanced. The ball changes from an object at rest to an object in motion.

motion in a straight line, unless it is compelled to change that state by forces impressed upon it." This means that an object—such as a ball tossed into the air—will continue to move unless there is some outside force that stops it. Along the same lines, if the ball is not moving, it will stay at rest unless some outside force moves it.

Some might say, "If Newton's first law were true, baseball players would be hitting home runs every time they stepped up to the plate. What's stopping the baseball from going into outer space?" Newton's first law seems strange when thought of in practical, everyday life, but it's actually quite accurate. Using the example of a fly ball in baseball, the ball is kept from traveling in a straight line into outer space forever by gravity. Gravity is a force. Newton's first law states that it is one of the "forces impressed upon" the baseball. Another force that presses on the ball is air, or air resistance. The air resistance slows the ball down. And to a lesser degree, friction, or the air passing over the ball, slows the ball down, too.

Along the same lines, one might ask, "Newton's first law also states that objects at rest will stay at rest. Then how come when I put a basketball down on a flat driveway, the ball rolls away?" Here again, gravity is the force causing the ball to roll down the slope of the driveway. Although the driveway may appear flat, the slightest angle will allow gravity to pull the ball toward the bottom of the slope. As gravity is pulling down on the ball, the ball will move down the driveway.

Here on Earth, there are a lot of forces acting on every object. At a glance, Newton's first law doesn't seem realistic. But consider this: in outer space, the force of gravity is much weaker, and there is no friction. So, a hit baseball would travel forever unless it ran into an object or fell into the gravitational pull of a planet, star, or some other celestial object. To illustrate this, the *Pioneer 11* spacecraft was launched in 1973 and traveled into deep space to take pictures of the outer solar system. Although the mission is now officially complete and all the craft's fuel and resources have been depleted, the spacecraft continues to travel through space because there's nothing to stop it—no friction, no gravity. In fact, the first star it will pass is in the constellation Aquila. But that won't be for a while, roughly 4 million years!

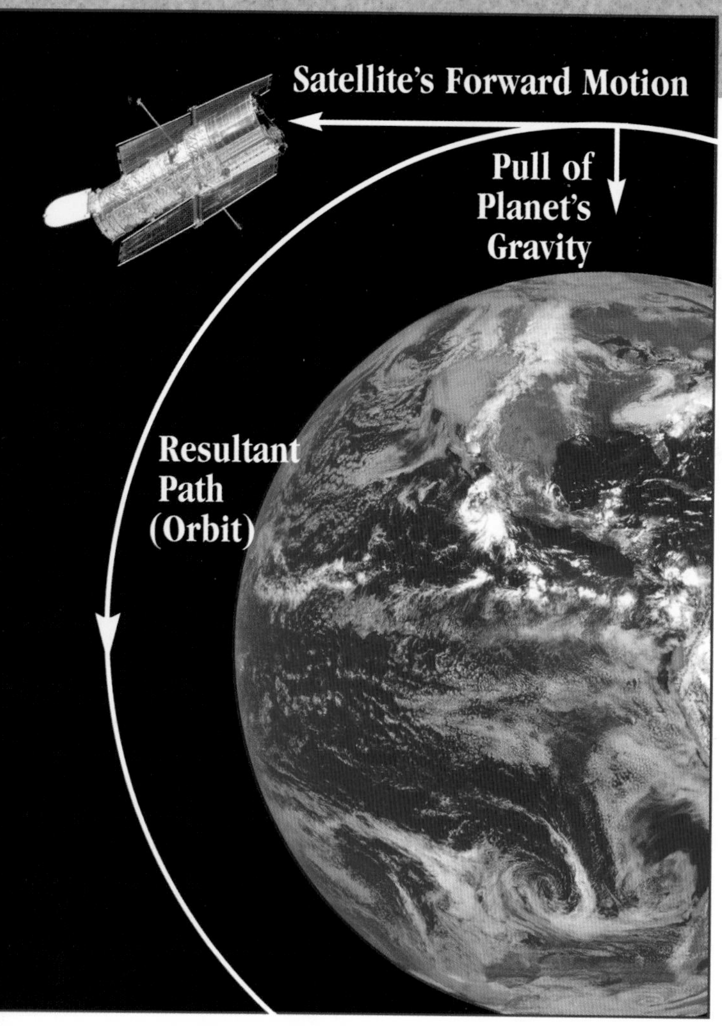

Space exploration has benefited from the practical application of Newton's first law of motion. Space probes are constantly demonstrating Newton's first law. Since there is very little friction in space, space probes can literally travel forever because objects in motion tend to stay in motion. However, their trajectories can change if acted upon by an outside force. In outer space, this force can be the gravitational pull of planets. This gravitational pull will curve the trajectory of the spacecraft, causing the craft to orbit the planet. The orbit is the combination of the spacecraft's forward motion and the planet's gravitational pull. Unless an outside force changes the direction of the spacecraft, it will orbit the planet forever.

The Second Law

Newton's second law of motion is a little more difficult to explain than the first. Simply stated, it is this: the change in motion of a body is proportional to the force pressed upon it. As an example, this law can be applied to pedaling a bicycle. The harder one pedals—pedaling is the force pressed upon the bicycle—the faster the bike will increase its speed.

Newton's second law is expressed in the following equation:

$$a = F/m$$

Here, "a" is acceleration, "F" is force, and "m" is mass. Acceleration is the change in the velocity of the bike over time. If one starts out at 0 miles per hour (0 km per hour) and crosses the finish line at 10 mph (16 km/h), then he or she has accelerated 10 mph (16 km/h):

End Speed – Start Speed ÷ Time = Acceleration

(10 mph [16 km/h] – 0 mph [0 km/h]) ÷ 1 minute = 10 mph (16 km/h) per minute

The force in the equation is that with which one pedals the bike. The mass is the weight of the bicycle plus the rider's weight.

So here, acceleration equals the force with which the bike is pedaled divided by the mass, or weight, of the bike and the person on the bike. So, if the acceleration is 11 mph per minute, this means that either the bike was pedaled harder or the rider and the bike weigh less. If the acceleration is 9 mph per minute, either the rider has not pedaled as hard or he or she and the bike weigh more.

Another way to see this equation is:

F = ma

In this equation, force (F) equals mass (m) multiplied by acceleration (a). This means that if the rider pedals harder, he or she will either accelerate at a faster rate or accelerate the same amount if the weight of the rider and bike is heavier. Imagine that after the race, one of the rider's friends wants a ride home on the bike. This increases the mass. So, in order to accelerate 10 mph (16 km/h) per minute, he or she would have to increase the force with which the bike is pedaled. In essence, the rider would have to pedal harder. One might say, "Of course I would have to pedal harder if I had a friend riding on the handle bars!" After all these numbers and fancy equations, Newton's laws boil down to basic common sense.

Newton's third law of motion simply states that every action has an equal and opposite reaction. Again, Newton's law is valuable to space exploration. When a rocket leaves a launchpad, it expels gas from its engine, an action otherwise known as thrust. The rocket pushes on the gas and the gas pushes on the rocket, allowing the craft to lift off and venture into outer space. The same law applies to an action as simple as riding a skateboard. The action (thrust) applied to the skateboard will produce an equal and opposite reaction that will propel the skateboard.

Newton's second law not only applies to riding a bicycle. The equation is used to calculate everything from the amount of fuel needed for race cars to the orbital paths of the planets. Yes, the same formula used to determine how fast a person can go on a bike is used to calculate the position of Jupiter, or any other object in space, at any given time.

The Third Law

Newton's third law is simply stated, but a little harder to imagine. It states that for every action, there is an equal and opposite reaction. This means that for any type of force pressed on a body (action), an equal force will be pressed back on that body (reaction). So, if a boy pushes his friend on a swing, the friend's back is pushing against the boy with the same amount of force with which he was just pushed. When the boy pushes his friend, the boy might be pushed back a bit himself. The reason for this is that the friend is able to move more easily on the swing than the boy with his feet planted firmly on the ground.

This law applies to every force we encounter every day. Standing on the sidewalk, your weight of 100 pounds (45 kilograms) is pressing down on the sidewalk. But this law says that the sidewalk is also pressing up against your feet with the equal force of 100 pounds (45 kg) even though it isn't moving. Yes, it's confusing, but imagine this: if the sidewalk wasn't pressing against you with equal force, you'd fall right through it as if the sidewalk were made of paper.

For example, find a friend and push against his or her shoulders while facing each other. Have him push against your shoulders in the same way. If you both push with equal force, neither of you will move backward. Even though you are locked motionless, you are still pushing against one another with a certain amount of force. The sidewalk pushes against you in the same way when you stand on it.

Newton's third law of motion can also be applied to the mechanics of airplanes. The wings lift the plane off the ground. The wings are designed to allow air to exert a certain amount of force beneath them. The amount of force that the air exerts on the bottom of the wings is equal to the weight of the plane. When the force of air is greater than the weight of the plane, the plane goes up. When the force of the air is less, the plane goes down. We see this principle in all of life. The paddling of a

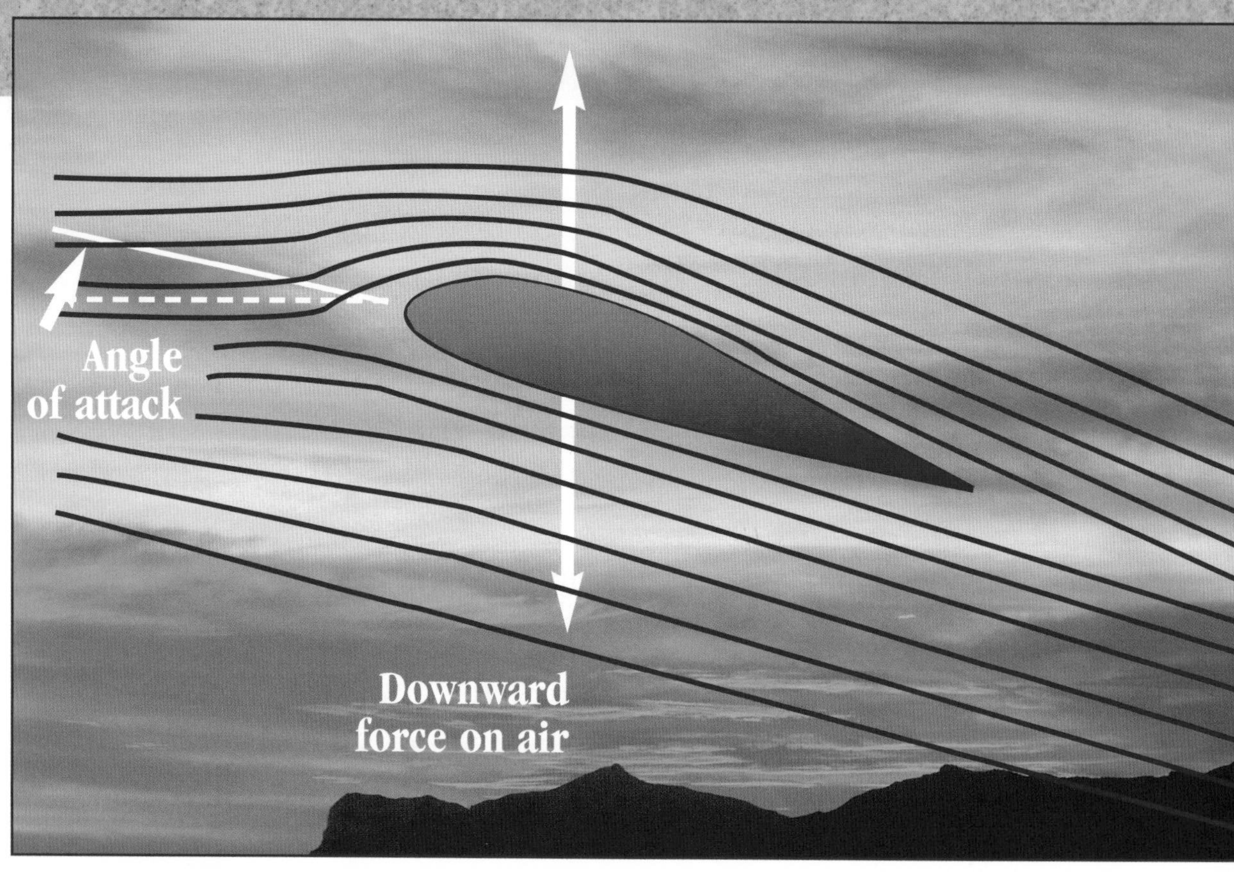

Newton's laws can also be applied to aerodynamics, a branch of science that deals with the motion of air and the forces acting on objects. This diagram demonstrates how Newton's third law helps a plane lift off and stay airborne. In the cross section in the diagram above, the flow of air moves left to right over a plane's wing. While the air flows above and below the wing, the shape of the wing forces the air traveling over the wing to travel a longer distance. This makes the air above the wing move faster. Faster air will create weaker air pressure. Therefore, the air below the wing has greater air pressure. This allows the wing to press up into the air because there is less pressure above the wing. Finally, the wing—and plane—lift off. This process is also known as Bernoulli's principle.

rowboat, the flight of a Frisbee, and the hitting of a golf ball all apply Newton's third law of motion. It can be seen everywhere. Along with the other two laws of motion and the law of gravity, it is universal.

CHAPTER 6

NEWTON'S UNIVERSALITY

Newton's scientific discoveries have come to be known simply as Newtonian physics—the study of the transfer of energy from one body to another in the universe. As discussed in the previous chapter, the first law states that force is needed to create a change in movement. The second law explains how much energy is needed to create a change in movement. And the third law shows how energy is exerted upon bodies in the universe. But Newton took into account only what he could see. He never imagined that his physics would affect so many aspects of life.

The Missing Planet

It is impossible to calculate just how much influence Newton has had on our understanding of the universe. Discoveries made through the use of his three laws have influenced other discoveries. Those discoveries have influenced yet other discoveries. Beginning with his three laws of motion, Newton started a domino effect of scientific discovery that continues today and will continue well into the future.

Immediately following the publication of the *Principia*, Newton put his newfound discoveries to work. For several years, he had been trying to calculate Saturn's orbit around the

The influence of Sir Isaac Newton continues to shape our understanding of the farthest reaches of the solar system and beyond. Today, Newton's theory of universal gravitation guides the work of scientists studying planetary orbits. Applying Newton's theory of universal gravitation toward existing planetary orbits has led to the discovery of new planets. Only time will tell what effect Newton's laws will have on studying other solar systems.

sun, though somewhat unsuccessfully. Saturn has an unusual orbit. Unlike the other planets in our solar system, Saturn does not follow a clear elliptical path that would appear to be caused by the gravitational influence of the sun on the planet. Instead, it moves somewhat erratically. Newton knew that the reason for this was that the path of Saturn was not only influenced by the sun but also by a closer, massive body such as the planet Jupiter. Jupiter influenced Saturn's gravity and ultimately the planet's orbit. Newton called Jupiter's influence on Saturn's orbit the "three-bodied problem."

Many years later, the planet Uranus, too, was seen to have an erratic orbital path much like that of Saturn. With Uranus, though, scientists could not see a celestial body whose gravity could be influencing the planet's orbital path. There must have been a planet there that they couldn't see. There was a planet out there that was, in effect, missing. Scientists John Couch Adams and Urbain-Jean-Joseph Le Verrier made the calculations, applied Newton's laws, and in 1846, discovered the planet Neptune.

Today, the use of mathematics with the understanding of the influence of one body on another is a common means of discovering celestial objects.

Tony Hawk's 900°

Using a more down-to-earth example, Newton's laws can also be applied to today's extreme sports. At the 1999 Summer X Games skateboard competition, professional skateboarder Tony Hawk, for the first time ever, landed what was regarded as the hardest trick in the entire sport: the 900°, two and a half rotations in mid-air off a half-pipe. Previously, Hawk had accomplished a 540° turn (one and a half rotations), even the 720° (two rotations). But the 900° was considered almost impossible because it required that Hawk turn the 900° in essentially the same amount of time in the air in which he before completed the 540° and 720°.

The X Games crowd was stunned when it saw him pull off and land the 900° after many attempts. Since change of motion is proportional to the force impressed upon it, Hawk had to increase the force he impressed in the direction in which he turned. This increase in force allowed him to turn at a greater velocity. Since he was turning at a greater velocity, he knew he could complete the two and a half rotations in the limited amount of time he had in the air. As Hawk successfully landed the 900°, the crowd roared with amazement. Whether he knew it or not, Hawk once again proved Newton's second law of motion.

The Return of the Comet

The discovery of Halley's comet can also be attributed to Newton. Comets had always been somewhat of a mystery to scientists because of their irregular movement across the sky. Halley's comet, however, has an unusually regular path. It orbits Earth approximately every seventy-six years. Unlike planets, which have more of a circular orbit, comets tend to move in sharp elliptical, or oval, orbits. Newton demonstrated that the movements of comets are subject to the same laws that control the planets in their orbits.

Edmond Halley always admired Newton. In fact, he wrote that Newton deserved the "admiration of the best Geometers and Naturalists, in this and all succeeding ages." Intrigued with Newton's discoveries, Halley wished to apply the scientist's calculations to a comet he observed in 1682. In studying this particular comet, Halley found that it had also been spotted before, once in 1531 and again in 1607.

Halley learned that the comet was seen even earlier, with its most famous appearance occurring in 1066, right before the Battle of Hastings. Historians through the ages have recorded that William of Normandy (also known as William the Conqueror) claimed the comet was a sign that he would

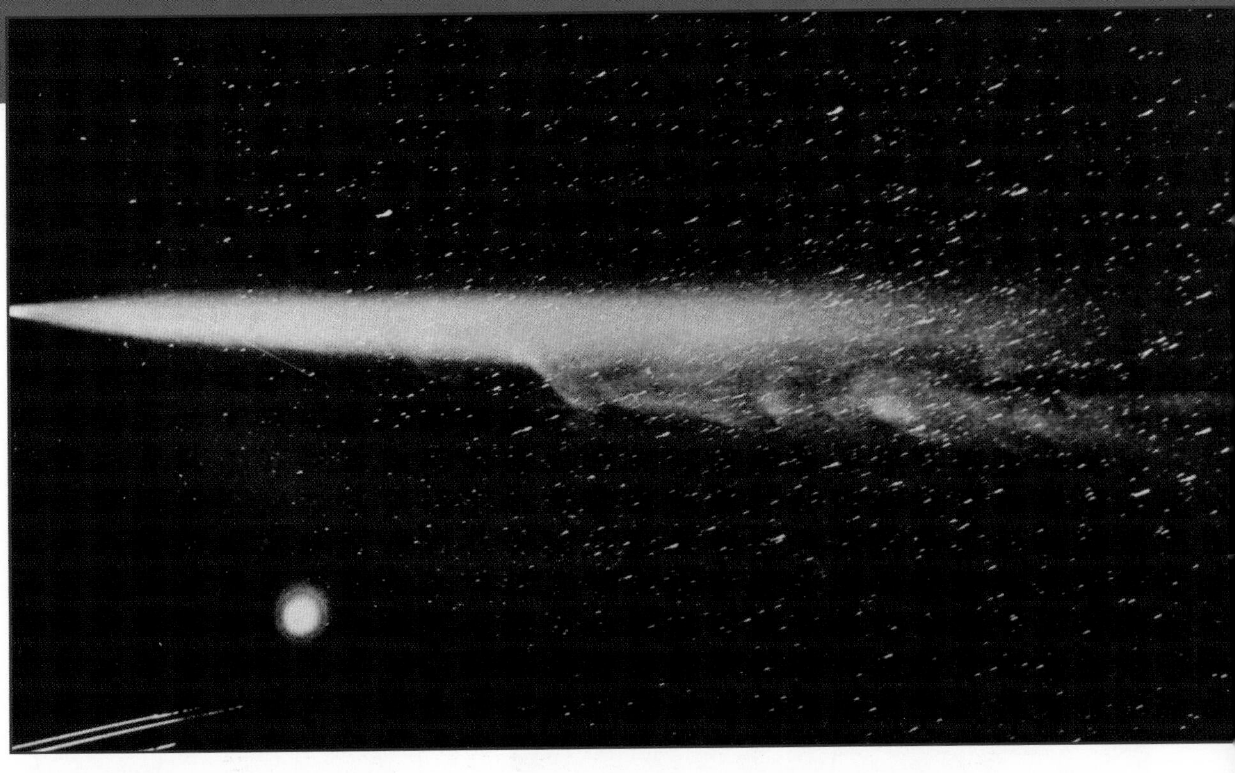

Sir Isaac Newton and Edmond Halley were colleagues, and their theories and discoveries are forever linked as well. Halley used Newton's laws to explain the return of a peculiar comet, which would become known as Halley's comet (pictured). By applying Newton's laws, Halley was able to calculate the comet's orbit. From that, he was able to predict when the comet would appear—every seventy-six years. In 1705, Halley used Newton's law of gravitation to predict the orbit of comets recorded in history. Through research, Halley found that a bright comet had passed Earth in 1531, 1607, and again in 1682. Unfortunately, Halley died in 1742 and never saw the return of the comet, which he had predicted. On Christmas night, 1758, a bright comet reappeared, just as Halley predicted it would. Halley's comet last passed Earth in 1986 and will do so again in 2061.

be victorious in battle over King Harold II of England. The battle was won by the Normans. Thus, some believe that the comet helped establish the Normans as rulers of England.

Halley thought, "Could this comet be orbiting the sun?" It appeared to be returning, passing Earth on a regular basis. To determine the next time the comet would pass Earth, Halley

Newton is generally regarded as the most original and influential theorist in the history of science. The influence of Sir Isaac Newton is immeasurable. From your backyard to the far corners of the universe, everything is affected by the laws Newton first put forth in the seventeenth century. Few have made as great a contribution as Newton. The spirit of Sir Isaac Newton exemplified the Scientific Revolution during the seventeenth and eighteenth centuries. Outside of science, the irrepressible mind of Newton also delved into theology, prophecy, and history. It was his passion and desire to unite knowledge and belief, to challenge what is accepted and prove it right or wrong.

applied Newton's laws of motion. His calculations revealed that the comet would return around the year 1758. Halley's comet did return in 1758, on Christmas Day, 116 years after the birth of Isaac Newton.

TIMELINE

1543 — Polish astronomer Nicolaus Copernicus argues that Earth is not, in fact, the center of the universe.

1609 — Johannes Kepler publishes his book *Astronomia Nova* (New Astronomy), which states that the planets move in elliptical rather than circular orbits around the sun.

1610 — Galileo observes four moons orbiting Jupiter in January and describes his findings in his book *Sidereus Nuncius* (The Sidereal Messenger).

1630 — Galileo completes *Dialogo Sopra i Due Massimi Sistemi del Mondo, Tolemaico e Copernicano* (Dialogue Concerning the Two Chief World Systems, Ptolemaic and Copernican).

1642 — Isaac Newton is born in Woolsthorpe, Lincolnshire, England, on Christmas Day.

1661 — Newton arrives at Trinity College in Cambridge, England.

1664 — Newton publishes his book of philosophical questions titled *Quaestiones Quaedam Philosophicae* (Certain Philosophical Questions).

TIMELINE *(continued)*

1665 — Newton graduates from Trinity College with a bachelor's degree.

1669 — Newton summarizes his findings on calculus in the paper titled *De Analysi per Aequationes Numeri Terminorum Infinitas* (On Analysis by Infinite Series).

1675 — Newton writes *An Hypothesis Explaining the Properties of Light.*

1678 — Newton suffers a nervous breakdown.

1679 — Newton completes his outline on the three laws of motion and universal gravitation, ideas that would lead to his landmark work *Philosophiae Naturalis Principia Mathematica* (Mathematical Principles of Natural Philosophy), commonly known as the *Principia*.

1684 — Newton sends Edmond Halley the first copy of *De Motu Corporum in Gyrum* (On the Motion of Revolving Bodies).

1686 — Newton presents to the Royal Society the first third of his manuscript *De Motu Corporum in Gyrum*.

1687 — *Philosophiae Naturalis Principia Mathematica* is published.

1696 — Newton accepts the post of warden of the British Royal Mint.

1703 — Newton is elected president of the Royal Society.

1704 — *Opticks* is published.

1705 — Newton is knighted for his scientific achievements by Queen Anne of Great Britain.

1706 — Newton publishes a Latin edition of *Opticks*.

1718 — Newton publishes a second English edition of *Opticks*.

1727 — Newton dies on March 20, in London.

PRIMARY SOURCE TRANSCRIPTIONS

Page 13: Excerpt from *Philosophiae Naturalis Principia Mathematica*

Transcription

Definitions

Definition I

The quantity of matter is the measure of the same, arising from its density and bulk conjointly.

Thus air of a double density, in a double space, is quadruple in quantity, in a triple space, sextuple in quantity. The same things are to be understood of snow, and fine dust or powders, that are condensed by compression or liquefaction, and all bodies that are by any causes whatever differently considered. I have no regard in this place to a medium, if any such there is, that freely pervades the interstices between the parts of bodies. It is this quantity that I mean hereafter everywhere under the name of body or mass. And the same is known by the weight of each body, for it is proportional to the weight, as I have found by experiments on pendulums, very accurately made, which shall be shown hereafter.

Page 25: Title page from *On Analysis by Infinite Series*

Transcription

The Method of Fluxions and Infinite Series;
With its Application to the Geometry of Curve-Lines.
By the Inventor
Sire Isaac Newton
Late President of the Royal Society
Translated from the Author's Latin Original not yet made publick.
To which is subjoin'd, A Perpetual Comment upon the whole Work,
consisting of Annotations, Illustrations, and Supplements,
In order to make this Treatise
A compleat Institution for the use of Learners.
By John Colson, M.A. and F.R.S.
Master of Sire Joseph Williamson's free Mathematical-School at Rochester.
London:
Printed by Henry Woodfall;
And Sold by John Nourse, at the Lamb without Temple-Bar.

Page 32: Excerpt from *Philosophiae Naturalis Principia Mathematica*

Transcription

this X the length which in the whole time V + W the comet might describe with that velocity which it has in the mean distance of the earth from the sun, which length is to be found by Cor. III, Prop. XI, Book III; and tV a perpendicular upon the chord Tt. In the mean observed longitude tB take at pleasure the point B, for the place of the comet in the plane of the ecliptic; and from thence, towards the sub S, draw the line BE, which may be to the perpendicular tV as the product of SB and St is to the cube of the hypothenuse of the right-angled triangle whose sides are SB and the tangent of the latitude of the comet in the second observation to the radius tB. And though the point E (by Lem. VII) draw the right line AEC, whose parts AE and EC, terminating in the right lines TA and tC, may be one to the other as the time V and W: then A and C will be nearly the places of the comet in the plane of the ecliptic in the first and third observations, if B was its place rightly assumed in the second.'

GLOSSARY

acceleration The rate of change of velocity over a period of time.

algebra A branch of mathematics that attempts to find the relationship between abstract numbers.

celestial Of or from the sky.

constant Continually occurring; having the same value everywhere.

contrary In opposition to.

counterfeiter Someone who creates fake money in hopes of profiting from its use.

ellipse An oval.

fluxions The name Newton gave to his branch of mathematics, which eventually became known as calculus.

focus One of two fixed points that forms the center of an ellipse.

force Exerted energy.

friction A force that prevents movement of one body past another.

geocentric Relating to a planetary system with Earth as its center.

geometry A branch of mathematics that deals with spatial relations.

gravity A force that affects all objects in the universe.

heresy Speaking or acting against certain religious beliefs.

impress To apply pressure.

inverse Opposite.

law A scientific principle that is proved to be true.

mass The amount of material an object contains.

mutual Sharing characteristics.
orbit The path one body takes around another.
prism A specially cut piece of glass designed to separate a beam of light into its individual colors.
product The result of two numbers being multiplied.
proportional The relation of the part to the whole.
spectrum A range of color formed when a beam of light is broken into its individual color elements.
square The product of a number multiplied by itself.
theory A scientific principle that is believed to be true but has not been proven.
universality Applying to everyone and everything.
velocity The rate of motion in a particular direction.

FOR MORE INFORMATION

Isaac Newton Institute for Mathematical Sciences
20 Clarkson Road
Cambridge, England
CB3 0EH
+440 1223 335999
e-mail: info@newton.cam.ac.uk
Web site: http://www.newton.cam.ac.uk

Jet Propulsion Laboratory
California Institute of Technology
4800 Oak Grove Drive
Pasadena, CA 91109
(818) 354-4321
Web site: http://www.jpl.nasa.gov

Smithsonian Institution Information
P.O. Box 37012
SI Building, Room 153, MRC 010
Washington, DC 20013-7012
e-mail: info@si.edu
Web site: http://www.si.edu

Web Sites

Due to the changing nature of Internet links, the Rosen Publishing Group, Inc., has developed an online list of Web sites related to the subject of this book. This site is updated regularly. Please use this link to access the list:

http://www.rosenlinks.com/psrsdt/ntlm

FOR FURTHER READING

Anderson, Margaret J. *Isaac Newton: The Greatest Scientist of All Time* (Great Minds of Science). Springfield, NJ: Enslow Publishers, 1996.
Berlinski, David. *Newton's Gift: How Sir Isaac Newton Unlocked the System of the World*. New York: Free Press, 2000.
Gleit, James. *Isaac Newton*. New York: Pantheon Books, 2003.
Parker, Barry. *The Isaac Newton School of Driving: Physics and Your Car*. Baltimore: Johns Hopkins University Press, 2003.
White, Michael. *Isaac Newton: Discovering Laws that Govern the Universe* (Giants of Science). Woodbridge, CT: Blackbirch Marketing, 1999.

BIBLIOGRAPHY

Christianson, Gale E. *Isaac Newton and the Scientific Revolution*. New York: Oxford University Press, 1996.

Encyclopædia Britannica. "Galileo." Retrieved February 19, 2004 (http://search.eb.com/eb/article?eu=108035).

Encyclopædia Britannica. "Robert Hooke." Retrieved February 19, 2004 (http://search.eb.com/eb/article?eu=41878).

Encyclopædia Britannica. "Sir Isaac Newton." Retrieved February 18, 2004 (http://search.eb.com/eb/article?eu=115657).

Gleick, James. *Isaac Newton*. New York: Pantheon Books, 2003.

NASA Glenn Learning Technologies Project. "Newton's Three Laws of Motion." January 2004. Retrieved January 2004 (http://www.grc.nasa.gov/WWW/K-12/airplane/newton.html).

"Newtonian Physics." January 2004. Retrieved January 2004 (http://zebu.uoregon.edu/~js/glossary/newtonian.html).

University of Chicago. "Lecture #9, May 1, 2003." May 1, 2003. Retrieved February 19, 2004 (http://www.astro.uchicago.edu/classes/natsci/102/spring-2003/lecture_notes/lecture9.pdf).

University of Oregon. "Dr. Darkmatter Presents the Electronic Universe: University of Tennessee. Astronomy 161: The Solar System." January 2004. Retrieved January 2004 (http://csep10.phys.utk.edu/astr161/lect/history/newton3laws.html).

PRIMARY SOURCE IMAGE LIST

Title page: Isaac Newton's manuscripts on optics and color, and the prism he used for these experiments. The photograph is by Erich Lessing. Newton's manuscript and prism are housed at Trinity College in Cambridge, England.
Page 5: Photograph by Erich Lessing of Isaac Newton's worktable at his home in Woolsthorpe, England.
Page 8: Oil-on-canvas painting by Hermann Goldschmidt done in 1847 after an earlier painting done by Sir Godfrey Kneller. Housed at the Academie des Sciences, Paris, France.
Page 9: Photograph by John Bethell of the Great Court at Trinity College, Cambridge, England.
Page 11: Newton's first telescope and manuscript pages of the *Principia*, photographed by Jim Sugar.
Page 13: Photograph of the cover page of a 1687 first edition printing of Isaac Newton's *Principia*. Today it is housed at Georgetown University, Washington, D.C.
Page 18: This hand-colored engraving done by an unknown artist in the sixteenth century is entitled *Planisphærium Copernicanum*. The piece is housed at the British Museum, London, England.
Page 20: This drawing of Galileo Galilei was done by Ottavio Mario Leoni in the early seventeenth century. It is housed at the Biblioteca Marucelliana in Florence, Italy.
Page 21: This photograph, by Gustavo Tomsich, shows one of Galileo's telescopes that he used in the seventeenth century. Today, the telescope is housed at the Museo di Storia della Scienza in Florence, Italy.
Page 25: This is the title page from the *Analysis per Quantitatum Series*, which was first published in 1711 and contained both of Newton's groundbreaking works, *De Analysi per Aequationes Numeri Terminorum Infinitas* (On Analysis by Infinite Series) and *De Methodis Serierum et Fluxionum* (On the Methods of Series and Fluxions).
Page 27: Pen-and-ink notebook page handwritten by Sir Isaac Newton, ca. 1669. Today, the page is housed at the Warden and Scholars of New College, Oxford, England.
Page 29: This digital simulation, done by artist David Seal, courtesy of NASA, depicts the flight path of the *Cassini* probe as it makes its way around Saturn.
Page 32: Proposition 41, Problem 21, from the first edition of Newton's *Principia*, 1687.
Page 34: An oil-on-canvas painting by Sir James Thornhill, 1710. The painting is now housed at Trinity College, Cambridge, England.
Page 35: A copper engraved print by an unknown artist, circa 1790. The engraving shows Gresham College before it was taken down to build a new excise office.
Page 46: A depiction of the solar system by artist Vincent Chaix entitled *The Solar System*.
Page 49: A photograph of Halley's comet taken May 13, 1910, by an unknown photographer in Flagstaff, Arizona.
Page 50: Oil-on-canvas painting by Sir Godfrey Kneller, 1702.

INDEX

O

P

Q

R

S

T

U

W

Photo Credits

Cover courtesy of the Royal Institution, London, UK/Bridgeman Art Library; title page, p. 5 Erich Lessing/Art Resource, NY; p. 8 Academie des Sciences, Paris, France/Archives Charmet/ Bridgeman Art Library; p. 9 John Bethell/Bridgeman Art Library; p. 11 © Jim Sugar/Corbis; pp. 13, 32 Science Museum/ Science & Society Picture Library; p 18 © Stefano Bianchetti/ Corbis; p. 20 Biblioteca Marucelliana, Florence/Bridgeman Art Library; p. 21 © Gustavo Tomsich/Corbis; p. 25 Science, Industry and Business Library, the New York Public Library; p. 27 courtesy of the Warden and Scholars of New College, Oxford/Bridgeman Art Library; p. 29 courtesy NASA/JPL-Caltech; p. 34 Trinity College, Cambridge, UK/Bridgeman Art Library; pp. 38, 42 Nancy Opitz; p. 40 courtesy NASA; p. 46 Vincent Chaix/Photo Researchers, Inc.; p 49 Lowell Observatory Archives; p. 50 Petworth House, West Sussex, UK/Bridgeman Art Library.

About the Author

Nicholas Croce is the author of *Detectives: Life Investigating Crime*. His writing has appeared in the *Bergen News*, the *New York Times*, and the literary magazine *Conceptions Southwest*.

Editor: Charles Hofer; Photo Researcher: Jeffrey Wendt

Markham Public Libraries
Milliken Mills Library
7600 Kennedy Road, Unit 1
Markham, ON L3R 9S5